Joe's nose

Story written by Liz Miles
Illustrated by Tim Archbold

Speed Sounds

Consonants

Ask your child to say the sounds (not the letter names) clearly and quickly, in and out of order. Make sure he or she does not add 'uh' to the end of the sounds, e.g. 'f' not 'fuh'.

Each box contains one sound. Focus sounds for this story are circled.

f ff ph	l ll le	m mm mb	n nn kn gn	r rr **wr**	s ss se **c** ce	v ve	z zz se **s**	sh	th	ng nk

b bb	c k ck	d dd	g gg gu	h	j g ge dge	p pp	qu	t tt	w wh	x	y	ch **tch**

Vowels

Ask your child to say the sounds in and out of order.

a	e ea	i	o	u	ay a-e a	ee ea y e	igh i-e ie i	ow o-e o oe
at	h**e**n	**i**n	**o**n	**u**p	d**ay**	s**ee**	h**igh**	bl**ow**

oo u-e ue	oo	ar	or oor ore aw	air are	ir ur er	ou ow	oy oi
z**oo**	l**oo**k	c**ar**	f**or**	f**air**	wh**ir**l	sh**ou**t	b**oy**

Story Green Words

For each word ask your child to read the separate sounds, e.g. 'b-u-s', 'p-oo-l' and then blend sounds together to make the word, e.g. 'bus', 'pool'. Sometimes one sound is represented by more than one letter, e.g. 'th', 'oo'. These are underlined.

clothes hose spoke wife doze Joe hurt whose*

Ask your child to say the syllables and then read the whole word.

take|a|way week|end a|bout bas|ket un|til so|fa

To|by groc|er|ies*

Ask your child to read the root first and then the whole word with the suffix.

rose → roses nod → nodded struggle → struggled

brag → bragged job → jobs get → getting lie → lied

happen → happening grow → grows long → longer

* Challenge Words

Vocabulary Check

Tell your child the meaning of each word in the context of the story.

	definition:	**sentence:**
chores	*little jobs at home*	*… Joe and his wife, Anya, had lots of chores to do.*
groceries	*food shopping*	*Anya had to go shopping for groceries.*
dozed	*slept for a short time*	*As Toby struggled with the wriggly hose, Joe dozed.*
twitched	*moved suddenly*	*Joe's nose twitched.*
snoozed	*had a short sleep*	*Mrs Lee piled the clothes in the basket as Joe snoozed.*
effort	*hard work*	*Cooking lunch was too much effort, so he rang for a takeaway.*
bragged	*showed off*	*It was fine until his mate bragged, "I went for a long run this morning."*

Red Words

Red words don't sound like they look. Ask your child to read the words but if he or she gets stuck read the word to your child.

old	all	could	are
water	my	through	son
want	one	ball	whole
people	now	once	anyone
over	was	two	some

Joe's nose

Do not read the story to your child first. Point to the words as your child reads. If your child gets stuck on a word help him or her say the sounds and blend them together. Re-read each sentence to your child to help him or her remember what he or she has read. Discuss what is happening on each page.

It was the weekend and Joe and his wife, Anya, had lots of chores to do. Anya had to go shopping for groceries. Joe had jobs too.

Joe lay on the sofa and looked at his list of chores. First he needed to water the roses.

“Toby, I’ve twisted my wrist,” Joe lied to his son. “Will you water the roses for me?”

Toby nodded. Joe’s nose itched.

As Toby struggled with the wriggly hose, Joe dozed.

Next on the list was getting the clothes in.

Joe spotted Mrs Lee next door.
“I've got a bad back, Mrs Lee. Please will you get the clothes off our line too?” he asked.

Joe's nose twitched.

Mrs Lee piled the clothes in the basket as Joe snoozed.

Then Joe needed to make lunch.

Cooking lunch was too much effort, so he rang for a takeaway.

"I've cooked lunch," Joe lied to Anya. And then his nose wiggled so much he ran to look in the mirror.

"Oh no! What's happening to my nose?" he gasped.

At football, Joe tried to hide his nose with his hand.

It was fine until his mate bragged, "I went for a long run this morning."

Joe said, "Me too!" and felt his nose grow. Now it was too long to hide.

Joe panicked and tried to run away, but he tripped on the ball.

“What’s happened to your nose?” Anya asked, when Joe got home.

Suddenly Joe realised what had happened: “I told some lies, and each time I lied my nose got longer and longer!

I said I had a bad wrist... but I didn’t.
I said I had a bad back... but I didn’t.
I said I cooked lunch... but I didn’t.
I said I went for a run... but I didn’t.

Then I tripped up. This time my back really does hurt!”

As he spoke, Joe's nose started to itch one more time. It began to shrink and soon it was back to the right size!

Toby sat next to Joe. "Daddy, please read this book to me. It's the one about a boy whose nose grows when he tells lies!"

Now ask your child to re-read the story helping him or her think about the best way to read each sentence.

Questions to talk about

Read the questions aloud to your child and ask him or her to find the answers on the relevant pages. Do not ask your child to read the questions – the words are harder than he or she can read at the moment.

p.9 What was the first job on Joe's list?

pp.10–11 Why did Joe lie to Toby and then to Mrs Lee?

p.12 Why was Joe's nose growing?

p.14 Which one of Joe's lies became true?

p.15 What made Joe's nose shrink back to its usual size?

p.15 What book does Toby want to read?

Questions to read and answer

Ask your child to read the questions and find the correct answer in the story.

1. **Anya / Toby / Mrs Lee** watered the roses for Joe.

2. When Mrs Lee was getting the clothes in, Joe **snoozed / helped / cooked lunch**.

3. When Joe looked in the mirror he saw that his nose **had shrunk / was the right size / had grown**.

4. Joe's mate told him that he had **been for a long run / watered the roses / hurt his wrist**.

5. Joe **kicked the football / was hit by the football / tripped on the football** when he tried to run away.

Speedy Green Words

Ask your child to read the words clearly and quickly – across the rows, down the columns, and in and out of order.

boy	nose	started	grows
right	away	please	door
too	read	home	hide
more	about	book	play
our	line	weekend	rang